JUST BE HAPPY
CROCHET HATS FOR BABIES AND TODDLERS

Alessandra Hayden

ISBN 978-0-578-07567-9

CONTENTS

ACKNOWLEDGEMENTS

I'd like to thank my husband Rob for believing in me, supporting my dreams and helping me watch our son Lucas while I crochet and design my patterns.

Also, I would like to thank the wonderful and kind pattern testers: Megan Aiken, Wendy Harbaugh and Debbie Alexander Procek.

Many thanks to my friends Marcia Terry, Sarah Van Wyhe, Holly Smith, Julie Van Zant, Carolyn Kipper and Jill Jones for allowing their precious kids to model the hats. Thanks to Carolyn for taking all the wonderful pictures and to Kamieo Fox for taking the picture of my son Lucas and me.

Last but not least, I owe a big thanks to Citlali Talina Contreras Moreno, my cyber–best friend; without her, this book wouldn't be possible.

I appreciate all the support and encouragement I received. Every time I thought about giving up, I had someone tell me I could do it, so thank you for helping me make this a reality.

And thank *you* for buying this book!

INTRODUCTION

My name is Alessandra and I was born in Marilia, a small town in the state of Sao Paulo, Brazil. Crochet has been my passion for most of my life: I learned to crochet from my grandma Dirce, my dad's mom. She taught me how to crochet using silk thread and a *very* small crochet hook; my first project was a clothes-hanger cozy.

Let me tell you, silk is tricky! But I didn't give up crocheting with that slippery thread and tiny hook, and I have never stopped crocheting in the more than twenty years since. I crocheted more often at some times than others, but I have never stopped.

I left Brazil when I got married and moved to the United States. After I had my son Lucas and became a stay-at-home mom and wife, I started crocheting more and selling my work online. I was used to working and making my own money, so crocheting was the perfect solution. It was a great way of making a little spending money of my own, and I was thrilled to be able to do something from home and raise my son at the same time.

At first I was making purses, scarves and afghans, but nothing was as fun as making kids' hats and trying them on my own little model. My son's colorful toys, his fun personality, and his big smile inspired me to create fun headwear. Soon people were asking me for more hats than any other product I made! Photographers, parents, family, everyone cherishes little ones, and a hat is a very nice way to add a blast of color and fun to a kid's outfit. After all, who doesn't smile at the sight of a little boy with a dinosaur hat? Or a girl in a flowered beanie?

In this book, I want to share some easy, cute hat patterns so you too can start making lovely, fun hats for the young ones you love! If you have little experience with crochet, let me assure you, it is a habit-forming, very flexible and easy-to-learn craft. If you are more experienced, I hope you will draw inspiration from my designs and let your imagination run free!

Cheers!

GENERAL GUIDELINES

Yarn

For every hat in this book I used worsted weight soft acrylic yarn, and in most cases, a size H/8 (5 mm) crochet hook. On rare occasions, a size I (5.5 mm) crochet hook was used.

Wonder why I chose acrylic? Well, there are many reasons: it's available in just about any color of the rainbow, it's very affordable, it's nonallergenic, and it's machine washable—with kids, you'll learn to appreciate the ease of care! Also, it won't shrink and nowadays, it's soft, not scratchy like it used to be. You should only buy good quality yarn if you want great hats that last long and look amazing.

If you want to use material other than acrylic, go ahead! But bear in mind that worsted weight should be used, no matter the fiber, if you want the hats to follow the sizes in the patterns. Also, if you chose wool, make sure it is superwash wool. This wool has been processed so it doesn't shrink if you machine wash it.

Most commercial yarns will not bleed or run when washed, but if you use hand-dyed yarns or some natural yarns, such as cotton, in dark colors, I'd recommend you do a test first: wash a swatch and place it on a white kitchen napkin while wet. Watch for coloring in the washing water and the napkin. You don't want to go through all the trouble of making a gorgeous, brightly colored hat to have the colors bleed and mix in the first wash!

Felt

I like using felt at times to give a specific look to a character that I create. Felt allows you to customize your hat, from adding features to a character to making a simple beanie pop with the addition of an initial in a contrasting color.

Be aware that there are several types of felt, some of which not meant to be washed and should not be used in clothing. I buy washable, 100% acrylic felt and make sure to test it for colorfastness. If you use wool felt, remember that it might shrink in the wash, so either wash the finished product by hand in cool water or skip the wool altogether.

Needle and thread

I like using a plastic yarn needle to embroider smiles. This type of needle is blunt and bends and seems not to pull the yarn. I also like using invisible thread to sew on the felt pieces; it's a little tricky to work with it, but once you get used to it, you will see that it's nice not to have to hide your stitches!

Stitch markers

When working in the round and not joining rounds, it is easy to lose the beginning of your round. Stitch markers will help you with that! A stitch marker can be anything from plastic rings to fancy premade stitch markers (you can find them in yarn or craft stores or from Etsy, if you'd like a lovely handmade one) to small amounts of contrasting yarn! Anything goes if it helps you keep your place. You will need them when you make hats with earflaps.

The following is a list of abbreviations used in this book and other crochet patterns

ch = chain
dc = double crochet
hdc = half double crochet
rnd = round (s)
rep = repeat
sc = single crochet
sk = skip
sl st = slip stitch
st(s) = stitch(es)
tr = treble (triple) crochet
tog = together

Gauge

4 rows x 7 hdc = 2 inch square

Gauge is always important if you want your garment to be the size indicated in the pattern. If you have no idea how to measure gauge, you should make a swatch piece at least 10 hdc wide and 10 rows high, wet it, and block it.

If you don't have a gauge ruler, get a piece of cardboard and cut a 2-inch square. Place it on top of the swatch and count how many rows (height) and hdc (width) are there in the square. If you have more rows or hdc than the gauge states, try going up a hook size; if you have less, go down a hook size. If the difference is minimal, try adjusting your tension (how tight or loose you crochet) until it matches the gauge.

REMEMBER! If you don't check your gauge, you might end up with a garment that is too big or too small, so why risk it?

HOW-TOS

Adjustable ring

This method of starting a crocheted piece in the round allows you to make a neat beginning with a practically nonexistent center hole. It's a very easy method.

Begin by making a loop of yarn, about half an inch in diameter. You want your "live" end of the yarn—the one taken from the skein—to be in the back of the loop. Hold it with your index finger while you insert your hook, grab the yarn and pull through it. Now you have a loop on your hook. Grab the yarn again with your hook and pull it through to complete a sc. From here on, add as many sc or hdc as are needed for your pattern.

In this book, you'll need to ch 2 then 7 hdc for each size of beanie. Once you've finished the round and start the next one, pull the loose end of the yarn to close the center hole.

Pom-pom

All the pom-poms I add to hats are hand crafted and measure about 2 ½ inches, but I must confess I cheat a little by using a pom-pom maker; it's such a time saver! If you can, get one. There are so many ways to use pom-poms to customize any garment; you can thank me later!

If you want to make pom-poms by hand, it is easy. You just need a sturdy piece of cardboard. It should be about 2 ½ inches wide; the length is not important. Fold it in half.

Start wrapping yarn tightly around the folded cardboard, but not so tightly that the cardboard folds! If you are making more than one pom-pom for a garment, you might want to count how many times you wrap the yarn so all pom-poms look the same. The more times you wrap the yarn, the thicker and fluffier the pom-pom you'll get!

Once you are happy with the amount of wraps, cut the wrapped yarn. Cut another piece of yarn and slip it between the halves of cardboard. Pull the yarn toward the opening in the cardboard and knot it very tightly around the wrapped yarn. Right and tight? Tie another knot, making sure it is secure, because these couple of knots are going to keep your pom-pom from coming undone.

Now that you've tied the wrapped yarn, cut the cardboard. If you wrapped it thickly, it may take several snips of the scissors, but don't worry if it looks shaggy. Once you've formed it you can tousle and trim it to your liking.

There! You have your pom-pom. Now you can make its twin if needed.

HEADS UP! Pom-poms and any ties can be choke hazards for your babies. Make sure they are all securely affixed to the hat so they are not easily removed. Pom-poms not to be used for hats for children under 3, if the children are to be unattended in the hat.

Basic Beanie Hats

Almost every hat is made in the same way: starting from a basic beanie and customizing it to make it unique.

Please read the instructions for each hat carefully, for even though they all start with the basic beanie, some have modifications that you will want to keep in mind as you make it (for example, the bee hat calls for a different-colored yarn in every round).

All hats are made in worsted weight yarn, using a crochet hook U.S. size H-8 (5 mm)

0–3 months (13–15-inch head circumference)

Foundation round (starting at the top of the hat): Make an adjustable ring; ch 2 and hdc 7 into ring. 8 hdc made.

Rnd 1: 2 hdc into each st (16 hdc made.)
Rnd 2: 2 hdc into next st, hdc into next st rep to end of rnd (24 hdc made)
Rnd 3: 2 hdc into next st, hdc into next 2 st, rep to end of rnd (32 hdc)
Rnd 4: 2 hdc into next st, hdc into next 3 st rep to end of rnd (40 hdc)
Rnd 5–12: hdc around. Fasten off.

3–6 months (15–17-inch head circumference)

Foundation round (starting at the top of the hat): Make an adjustable ring; ch 2 and hdc 7 into ring. 8 hdc made.

Rnd 1: 2 hdc into each st (16 hdc made.)
Rnd 2: 2 hdc into next st, hdc into next st, rep to end of rnd (24 hdc made)
Rnd 3: 2 hdc into next st, hdc into next 2 st, rep to end of rnd (32 hdc)
Rnd 4: 2 hdc into next st, hdc into next 3 st, rep to end of rnd (40 hdc)
Rnd 5: 2 hdc into the next st, hdc into next 19 sts, rep to the end of rnd (42 hdc)
Rnd 6–13: hdc around. Fasten off.

6–12 months (17–19-inch head circumference)

Foundation round (starting at the top of the hat): Make an adjustable ring; ch 2 and hdc 7 into ring. 8 hdc made.

Rnd 1: 2 hdc into each st (16 hdc)
Rnd 2: 2 hdc into next st, hdc into next st, rep to end of rnd (24 hdc)
Rnd 3: 2 hdc into next st, hdc into next 2 st, rep to end of rnd (32 hdc)
Rnd 4: 2 hdc into next st, hdc into next 3 st, rep to end of rnd (40 hdc)
Rnd 5: 2 hdc into the next st, hdc into next 9 sts, rep to the end of rnd (44 hdc)
Rnd 6–14: hdc around. Fasten off.

12–36 months (18–20-inch head circumference)

Foundation round (starting at the top of the hat): Make an adjustable ring; ch 2 and hdc 7 into ring. 8 hdc made.

Rnd 1: 2 hdc into each st (16 hdc)
Rnd 2: 2 hdc into next st, hdc into next st, rep to end of rnd (24 hdc)
Rnd 3: 2 hdc into next st, hdc into next 2 st, rep to end of rnd (32 hdc)
Rnd 4: 2 hdc into next st, hdc into next 3 st, rep to end of rnd (40 hdc)
Rnd 5: 2 hdc into next st, hdc into next 4 st, rep to end of rnd (48 hdc)
Rnd 6–16: hdc around. Fasten off.

Earflaps

Lay your hat flat, count 3 stitches in from each side and mark the spot with a stitch marker or piece of yarn.
You have just marked where your earflaps will go.
Join yarn at the first stitch marker. You will work toward the back of the hat.

Row 1: hdc 8 stitches (0–3- and 3–6-month hats) or 9 stitches (6–12- and 12–24-month hats). Ch 2, turn.
Row 2: Skip 1st hdc. In each hdc across, ch 2, turn (7 sts for 0–3- and 3–6-month hats, or 8 sts for 6–12- and 12–24-month hats).
Repeat Row 2 until there is just 1 hdc remaining, then ch 15 and attach pom-pom.

Trim

Join the desired color of yarn on back of the hat and single crochet evenly around the edge and earflaps, working 2 single crochets at the tip of each earflap.

Braids

Cut 18 20-inch strands of yarn and divide into 2 groups of 9 strands. Fold one group of 9 in half and push the folded end through the bottom space of the earflap. Pull both ends of each strand through the folded loop and pull up neatly, keeping the ends the same length. Braid these 18 strands gently and tie an overhand knot near the end. Repeat on the other side.

HATS

BEE

Buzzing through the garden, just as cute as can be
A flower's best friend: a little bumble bee.

Yarn requirements:

1 skein worsted weight in black
1 skein worsted weight in yellow

Basic beanie modifications

Choose the desired size of beanie and make odd-numbered rounds with black and even-numbered rounds with yellow. Fasten off and weave in ends.

Pom-poms

Using yellow yarn, make two 2 ½-inch pom-poms. Always attach pom-poms securely for the safety of your child!

Antennas (make 2)

Join black yarn at the top of the hat (on R1) ch 5, turn sl st in each chain, and attach pom-pom. Pom-poms will be free to move around!

BLUE BIRD

Blue bird, blue bird, flying so high,
Tell me, what do you see in the sky?

This hat is different from the others, not only because the character is different, but also because it's made in a square instead of a round beanie shape.

Yarn requirements

1 skein worsted weight in turquoise
Scraps of black, white and orange
1 skein of Fun Fur yarn to match the turquoise

Make the desired size of hat using one strand each of turquoise WW and Fun Fur together, then follow the instructions for face, eyes and beak.

Square hats

Hats are worked in continuous rounds; do not join.

0–3 months (13–15-inch head circumference)

Ch 22, turn.
Rnd 1: hdc in 3rd ch from hook, and in each st across (20 hdc). DO NOT turn. Continue hdc in each st on other side of starting chain. Do not join (40 hdc around).
Rnd 2–12: Continue working 1 hdc in each st continuously around.
Fasten off.

3–6 months (15–17-inch head circumference)

Ch 23, turn.
Rnd 1: hdc in 3rd CH from hook and in each st across (21 hdc), DO NOT turn. Continue hdc in each st on other side of starting chain. Do not join (42 hdc around).

Rnd 2–12: Continue working 1 hdc in each st continuously around.
Fasten off.

6–12 months (17–19-inch head circumference)

Ch 24, turn.
Rnd 1: hdc in 3rd ch from hook and in each st across (22 hdc). DO NOT turn. Continue hdc in each st on other side of starting chain. Do not join (44 hdc around).

Rnd 2–12: Continue working 1 hdc in each st continuously around.
Fasten off.

12–36 months (18–20-inch head circumference)

Ch 24, turn.
Rnd 1: hdc in 3rd ch from hook and in each st across (24 hdc). DO NOT turn. Continue hdc in each st on other side of starting chain. Do not join (48 hdc around).

Rnd 2–12: Continue working 1 hdc in each st continuously around.
Fasten off.

Beak (worked in rounds)

Rnd 1: Using orange yarn, ch 2, 3 sc in second ch from hook (3)
Rnd 2: 2 sc in each st (6)
Rnd 3: 2 sc in the same st, 1 sc in the next st, repeat around (9)
Rnd 4: 2 sc in the same st, 2 sc in the next 2 sts, repeat around (12)
Rnd 5: 2 sc in the same st, 3 sc in the next sts, repeat around. (15)
Fasten off, leaving a long tail. Stuff beak lightly with polyester fill.

Eyes (make 2)

Rnd 1: Using black yarn, ch 2, 7 sc in the 1st st from hook (7).
Rnd 2: Change to turquoise yarn. 2 sc in each st (14).

Rnd 3: Change to white yarn. Sl st around (21).
Fasten off, leaving a long tail to sew eyes to the hat.

Pom-poms

Using turquoise and black yarn, make two 2 ½-inch pom-poms. Always attach pom-poms securely for the safety of your child!

CHICKEN

Chickens can scratch and chickens can cluck,
Maybe this bright-eyed chicken will bring you good luck!

<u>Yarn requirements:</u>

1 skein worsted weight in white
Scraps of red, black, orange and yellow
Make the desired size of beanie in white, and then follow the directions below for earflaps, beak, eyes and comb.

Pom-poms

Using yellow yarn, make two 2 ½-inch pom-poms.

Earflaps

Lay your hat flat, count 3 stitches in from each side and mark the spot with a stitch marker or piece of yarn.

You have just marked where your earflaps will go.

Join yarn at the first stitch marker. You will work toward the back of the hat.

Row 1: hdc 8 stitches (0–3- and 3–6-month hats) or 9 stitches (6–12- and 12–24-month hats). Ch 2, turn.

Row 2: Skip 1st hdc. In each hdc across, ch 2, turn (7 sts for 0–3- and 3–6-month hats, or 8 sts for 6–12- and 12–24-month hats).

Repeat Row 2 until there is just 1 hdc remaining, then ch 15 and attach pom-pom.

Make 2nd earflap in the same manner as the first.

Eyes (make 2, worked in rounds)

Rnd 1: Using black yarn, ch 2, 6 hdc in the 1st st from hook (6).

Rnd 2: Change to white yarn. 2 hdc in each st (12).

Rnd 3: Change to black yarn. Sl st around (12).

Fasten off, leaving a long tail to sew eyes to the hat.

Beak

Using orange yarn, ch 7.

Row 1: sc in 2nd ch from hook and in each remaining st. Ch 1, turn (6).

Row 2: skip 1st sc, sc in each st across. Ch 1, turn (5).

Row 3–6: Repeat row 2, decreasing one sc each row until there is only on sc left.

Sc around the whole beak. Fasten off, leaving a long tail for sewing.

Comb

Row 1: Ch 19, sc in 2nd ch from hook and in each remaining st (18). Turn.

Row 2: 6 hdc in 3 sc. Sk 2 sc, sl st in next sc, sk 2 sc, 6 dc in next sc twice. Sl st in the last sc. Fasten off, leaving a long tail to sew comb to the hat.

Using a blunt tapestry needle, attach each piece to the hat using the picture as a guide.

CRAB

By the water of the sea, a cute crab there you will be.

Yarn requirements

1 skein worsted weight yarn in red
Red, white and black felt
Make the desired size of beanie. Follow the directions below for eyes, claws and earflaps.

Eyes (make 2)

Rnd 1: Ch 2, 6 sc in second ch from hook (6).
Rnd 2: 2 sc in each st (12).
Rnd 3: 2 sc in the same st, 1 sc in the next st, repeat around (18).
Fasten off, leaving a long tail for sewing eyes to hat.
Cut 2 circles out of white felt and 2 smaller circles out of black felt for pupils. Sew them to eyes with needle and thread, then sew eyes to the top of the hat, using the picture as a reference.

Earflaps

Lay your hat flat, count 3 stitches in from each side and mark the spot with a stitch marker or piece of yarn.
You have just marked where your earflaps will go.
Join yarn at the first stitch marker; you will work toward the back of the hat.

Row 1: hdc 8 stitches (0–3- and 3–6-month hats) or 9 stitches (6–12 and 12–24-month hats). Ch 2, turn.
Row 2: Skip 1st hdc. In each hdc across, ch 2, turn. (7 sts for 0–3- and 3–6-month hats, or 8 sts for 6–12- and 12–24-month hats.)
Repeat Row 2 until there are just 3 hdc remaining.
Add 4 or 5 more rows of 3 hdc each. Fasten off.
Make 2nd earflap in the same manner as the first.
Sc around the hat.
Add a button to one of the flaps for closure, if desired.

Claws (make 2)

Cut 4 pieces of red felt, using the claw template.
With needle and thread, sew 2 pieces together around the edges and stuff lightly with polyester fill. Repeat the process for the other 2 pieces. Sew claws to hat using the picture as a reference.

LADYBUG

Red as a rose, with striking black dots
The ladybug delights our gardens and hearts.

Yarn requirements

1 skein red worsted weight yarn
1 skein black worsted weight yarn
Make the desired size of beanie in red and the last 2 rows in black, and then follow the directions below for earflaps, dots, and antennae.

Earflaps (alternate method)

Lay your hat flat, count 3 stitches in from each side and mark the spot with a stitch marker or piece of yarn.

You have just marked where your earflaps will go.

Join yarn at the first stitch marker; you will work toward the back of the hat.

Row 1: hdc 8 stitches (0–3- and 3–6-month hats) or 9 stitches (6–12- and 12–24-month hats). Ch 2, turn.

Row 2: Skip 1st hdc. In each hdc across, ch 2, turn. (7 sts for 0–3- and 3–6-month hats or 8 sts for 6–12- and 12–24-month hats.)

Repeat Row 2 until there is just 1 hdc remaining. Ch 15. Fasten off and attach pom-poms.

Make 2nd earflap in the same manner as the first.

Pom-poms

Make 2 pom-poms about 2 ½ inches using red yarn. Always attach pom-poms securely for the safety of your child!

Spots (make 6)

With black yarn, ch 2.
Row 1: Work 6 sc in first ch.
Fasten off, leaving a long tail for sewing.

Antennae (make 2)

With black yarn, ch 2.
Row 1: Work 5 sc in first ch.
Row 2: Work 2 sc in each st around (10).
Row 3: Sc in each st around.
Row 4: Sc 2 tog around (5). Stuff firmly with polyester fill or black yarn.
Rows 5–7: Sc in each st around.

Fasten off, leaving a long tail for sewing.
Using a blunt tapestry needle, sew antennae to the top of the hat and sew spots around.

LION

This sweet little lion has a beautiful mane,
But don't let that trick you, for she might not be tame!

Yarn requirements:

1 skein worsted weight yarn in yellow
1 skein worsted weight yarn in orange
Make the desired size beanie with yellow yarn and follow instructions below for mane and ears.

Mane

Join orange yarn, make a loop, and start with 1 dc, ch 3. Sl st in the beginning of the first ch (the first of the 3 chains you just made).That forms a picot. Now 1 dc, 1 picot, 1 dc, 1 picot, 1 dc, 1 picot, 1 dc, 1 picot, 1 dc, 1 picot all in the same st. Skip 5 sts and repeat all the way around. Fasten off, weave in ends.

Note: the mane is made out of little bundles of ruffles that consist of 6 dc and one picot between each dc.

Ears (make 2 yellow and 2 orange)

Rnd 1: Ch 2, 6 sc in 2nd ch from hook (6).
Rnd 2: 2 sc in each st (12).
Rnd 3: 2 sc in the same st, 1 sc in the next st, repeat around (18).

Fasten off and weave in the ends of orange circles.
Place the orange circle on top of the yellow. With the crochet hook, sc through both thicknesses. Fasten off, leaving a tail to sew ear to hat. Repeat the same process for the other ear.
Using a blunt tapestry needle, sew ears to hat, cupping them a little bit, and weave in any loose ends.

LIZARD

Scaly and long, he moves really fast.
Don't blink, for this lizard will not come in last.

Yarn requirements

1 skein worsted weight yarn in green
1 skein worsted weight yarn in yellow
Small amounts of polyester fill
Small amount of red felt
Make the desired size of beanie. Follow the directions below for the spikes, earflaps and braids.
Spikes from large to small:

Spike 1 (largest)

Rnd 1: Ch 2, 3 sc in second ch from hook (3).
Rnd 2: 2 sc in each st (6).
Rnd 3: 2 sc in the same st, 1 sc in the next st, repeat around (9).
Rnd 4: 2 sc in the same st, 2 sc in each of the next 2 sts, repeat around (12).
Rnd 5: 2 sc in the same st, 3 sc in each of the next sts, repeat around (15).
Rnd 6: 2 sc in the same st, 4 in each of the next sts, repeat around (18).
Fasten off, leaving a long tail.

Spike 2 (make 2)

Repeat rounds 1–5 of spike 1. Fasten off, leaving a long tail.

Spike 3

Repeat rounds 1–4 of spike 1. Fasten off, leaving a long tail.

Spike 4 (smallest)

Repeat rounds 1–3 of spike 1. Fasten off, leaving a long tail.
Stuff spikes lightly with polyester fill and attach them to hat from largest to smallest, using the picture as guide.

Earflaps

Lay your hat flat, count 3 stitches in from each side and mark the spot with a stitch marker or piece of yarn.
You have just marked where your earflaps will go.
Join yarn at the first stitch marker; you will work toward the back of the hat.
Row 1: hdc 8 stitches (0–3- and 3–6-month hats) or 9 stitches (6–12- and 12–24-month hats). Ch 2, turn.
Row 2: Skip 1st hdc. In each hdc across, ch 2, turn. (7 sts for 0–3- and 3–6-month hats or 8 sts for 6–12- and 12–24-month hats.)
Repeat Row 2 until there are just 2 hdc remaining. Fasten off.
Make 2nd earflap in the same manner as the first.

Trim

Join yellow yarn and sc around.

Braids

Cut 18 20-inch strands of yarn and divide into 2 groups of 9. Fold one group of 9 in half and push the folded end through the bottom space of the earflap. Pull the ends of each strand through the folded loop and pull up neatly, keeping the two ends the same length. Braid these strands gently and tie an overhand knot near the end. Repeat on the other side.

Tongue

Cut a small rectangle out of red felt, cut a V, and sew the tongue to the front of the hat using invisible thread.

MONKEY

Swings from the trees, eats bananas all day,
We're sure this cute monkey has something to say!

Yarn requirements

1 skein worsted weight yarn in brown
1 skein worsted weight yarn in beige
Small amount of black yarn
Make the desired size beanie with brown yarn and follow instructions below for muzzle, ears and eyes.

Muzzle

Rnd 1: Using beige yarn, ch 13. Starting on the 3rd ch from the hook, hdc into each st until you get to the last ch. 3 hdc into the last chain and continue to hdc into each hdc down the other side of the chain (24 hdc).

Rnd 2: Sc around (24sc).

Fasten off, leaving a long tail for sewing the muzzle to the hat. Using black yarn, embroider a smile.

Ears (Make 2)

Rnd 1: Using beige yarn, ch 3, join to make a circle. 3 sc into the circle. Turn.

Rnd 2: 2 sc in the 1st sc, 1 sc in the next sc, 2 sc in the last sc. Turn. (5).

Rnd 3: 1 sc in 1st sc, 2 sc in the next 3 sc, 1 sc in last sc. Fasten off. (8).

Rnd 4: Using brown yarn, 2 sc into the 1st sc, 1 sc into each of the next 6 sts, 2 sc into the last sc. Turn. (10).

Rnd 5: Repeat round 4 (12). Fasten off, leaving a long tail for sewing ears to hat.

Note: Ears will look like pie slices, but don't worry, once you sew them to the hat, they will look perfect!

Eyes

Rnd 1: Using black yarn, ch 2, 6 sc in second ch from hook (6). Fasten off, leaving a long tail for sewing eyes to hat.

MOUSE

A mouse in your house, "No way!" you might say.
But this tiny one comes to brighten your day!

Yarn requirements

1 skein worsted weight yarn in charcoal gray
Small amount of worsted weight yarn in pink
Make the desired size beanie, but DO NOT FASTEN OFF. Follow the directions below for tail and ears.
Make a 2 ½-inch pom-pom out of gray yarn.

Tail

Ch 10. Fasten off and attach pom-pom. Always attach pom-poms securely for the safety of your child!

Ears (make 2 pink and 2 gray)

Rnd 1: Ch 2, 6 sc in second ch from hook (6).
Rnd 2: 2 sc in each st (12).
Rnd 3: 2 sc in the same st, 1 sc in the next st, repeat around (18).

Fasten off and weave in the ends of pink circles.
Place the pink circle on top of the gray. With the crochet hook, sc through both thicknesses. Fasten off, leaving a tail to sew ears to hat.
Using a blunt tapestry needle, sew ears to hat and weave in any loose ends.

PENGUIN

He wears a tuxedo without a bow tie
A cute little bird; too bad he can't fly.

Yarn requirements

1 skein worsted weight yarn in black
1 skein worsted weight yarn in white
Small amount of worsted weight yarn in orange
Make the desired size of beanie in black, then follow the directions below for earflaps, pom-poms, face, eyes and beak.

Earflaps

Lay your hat flat, count 3 stitches in from each side and mark the spot with a stitch marker or piece of yarn. You have just marked where your earflaps will go.

Join yarn at the first stitch marker; you will work toward the back of the hat.

Row 1: hdc 8 stitches (0–3- and 3–6-month hats) or 9 stitches (6–12- and 12–24-month hats). Ch 2, turn.

Row 2: Skip 1st hdc. In each hdc across, ch 2, turn. (7 sts for 0–3- and 3–6-month hats or 8 sts for 6–12- and 12–24-month hats).

Repeat Row 2 until there is just 2 hdc remaining. Fasten off.

Make 2nd earflap in the same manner as the first.

Pom-poms

Make 2 pom-poms about 2 ½ inches using white yarn. Always attach pom-poms securely for the safety of your child!

Face

Row 1: Ch 17, hdc in the 3rd st from hook, hdc in each remaining st. (15).

Row 2–7: hdc across (15).

Row 8: sk 3, 5 tr into 4th st, sl st into 8th st, skip 3 sts, 5 trc into 12th st, skip remaining sts and sl st into the 15th.

Sc around the whole face. Fasten off, leaving a long tail to sew face to beanie.

Beak

Rnd 1: Using orange yarn, ch 2, 3 sc in second ch from hook (3).

Rnd 2: 2 sc in each st (6).

Rnd 3: 2 sc in the same st, 1 sc in the next st, repeat around (9).

Rnd 4: 2 sc in the same st, 2 sc in the next 2 sts, repeat around (12).

Rnd 5: 2 sc in the same st, 3 sc in the next sts, repeat around (15).

Fasten off, leaving a long tail. Stuff lightly beak with polyester fill.

Eyes

Cut 2 small circles out of black felt and sew them to the face using invisible thread.

Hair

Cut three or four 6-inch lengths of black yarn, thread them through the top of the beanie, and make a knot.

PIG

Cute as can be, so wonderfully pink,
this little pig is quite sweet, don't you think?

Yarn requirements

1 skein worsted weight yarn in dark pink
1 skein worsted weight yarn in pale pink
Small amount of worsted weight yarn in black for smile and nostrils
Small amount of black felt for eyes
Make the desired size of beanie; follow the directions below for the ears, nose, earflaps and braids.

Ears (make 2)

Rnd 1: Ch 2, 3 sc in second ch from hook (3).
Rnd 2: 2 sc in each st (6).
Rnd 3: 2 sc in the same st, 1 sc in the next st, repeat around (9).
Rnd 4: 2 sc in the same st, 2 sc in the next 2 sts, repeat around (12).
Rnd 5: 2 sc in the same st, 3 sc in the next sts, repeat around (15).
Rnd 6–7: repeat round 5 (no increases).
Fasten off, leaving a long tail for sewing.

Nose

Rnd 1: Using dark pink, ch 3, hdc 6 in the 3rd ch from hook (7).
Rnd 2: 2 hdc in each hdc from previous round (14).
Cut small oval shapes from black felt and sew to face using invisible thread.
Using black yarn, embroider smile and nose nostrils.

Earflaps

Lay your hat flat, count 3 stitches in from each side and mark the spot with a stitch marker or piece of yarn.

You have just marked where your earflaps will go.

Join yarn at the first stitch marker; you will work toward the back of the hat.

Row 1: hdc 8 stitches (0–3- and 3–6-month hats) or 9 stitches (6–12- and 12–24-month hats). Ch 2, turn.

Row 2: Skip 1st hdc. In each hdc across, ch 2, turn. (7 sts for 0–3- and 3–6-month hats or 8 sts for 6–12- and 12–24-month hats.)

Repeat Row 2 until there is just 2 hdc remaining. Fasten off.

Make 2nd earflap in the same manner as the first.

Trim

Join dark pink yarn and sc around.

Braids

Cut 18 20-inch strands yarn and divide into 2 groups of 9. Fold one group of 9 in half and push the folded end through the bottom space of the earflap. Pull the ends through the folded loop and pull up neatly, keeping the two ends the same length. Braid these strands gently and tie an overhand knot near the end. Repeat on the other side.

TURTLE

Hard shell on top, soft body below,
A turtle might get there, but it's going to be slow.

Yarn requirements

1 skein worsted weight yarn in light green
1 skein worsted weight yarn in dark green
Small amount of white felt
Two 6 mm safety eyes or a small amount of black felt
Make desired size beanie in light green and change colors to dark green for the last 2 rounds.

Head and Legs:

Work in continuous rounds; do not join or turn.

Legs (make 4)

Rnd 1: Ch 2, 4 sc in the second chain from the hook.
Rnd 2: 2 sc into each st (8).
Rnd 3–5: sc around. Fasten off, leaving a long tail.

Head:

Rnd 1: ch 2, 6 sc in the second chain from the hook.
Rnd 2: sc into each st (12).
Rnd 3: 2 sc into next st, sc into next st, rep to end of rnd (18).
Rnd 4: 2 sc into next st, sc into next 2 sts, rep to end of rnd (24).
Rnd 5–7: sc around (24).
Rnd 8: sc 2 tog, sc in next 2 st, rep around (18).
Rnd 9: sc 2 tog, sc in next st, rep around (12). Fasten off, leaving a long tail to attach head to hat.

Cut 2 small circles out of white felt. Poke a little hole in the center to attach 6 mm safety eyes or cut smaller circles out of black felt. Sew to turtle's head using invisible thread. Stuff head firmly with polyester fill, sew to hat. Stuff legs firmly and sew to hat, using the picture as a guide.

CPSIA information can be obtained
at www.ICGtesting.com
Printed in the USA
LVIC040859211211

260460LV00004B